The Country Kitchen
HERBS
Anne Chapman

The Country Kitchen

HERBS

Anne Chapman

WELDON
PUBLISHING

Front and back of jacket: A basketful of fresh herbs gathered straight from a country garden in the early morning.

Front and back endpapers: An old-fashioned country kitchen with the preparation for a spicy fruit cake in the foreground. The wood fuel stove is wonderful for long, slow cooking.

Page 2: Pots of herbs grow happily on a wrought-iron stand against a sunny wall.

COOK'S NOTES: *Standard spoon and cup measurements are used in all recipes. All spoon and cup measurements are level.*

1 tablespoon = 20 ml spoon
1 teaspoon = 5 ml spoon
1 cup = 250 ml

As the imperial and metric equivalents are not exact, follow either one or the other system of measurements.

All ovens should be preheated to the specified temperature.

Fresh herbs are used unless otherwise stated. If they are unavailable, use half the quantity of dried herbs. Use freshly ground black pepper whenever pepper is used. Salt and pepper to your individual taste. Flour, unless stated otherwise, means plain flour.

A Kevin Weldon Production
Published by Weldon Publishing,
a division of Kevin Weldon & Associates Pty Ltd
372 Eastern Valley Way, Willoughby, NSW 2068 Australia

First published 1992

© Copyright Kevin Weldon & Associates Pty Ltd
© Copyright design: Kevin Weldon & Associates Pty Ltd

Publishing Manager: Robin Burgess
Project Coordinator: Barbara Beckett
Designer and illustrator: Barbara Beckett
Photographer: Ray Jarratt
Typeset in Hong Kong by Graphicraft Typesetters Ltd
Produced in Hong Kong by Mandarin Offset

National Library of Australia Cataloguing-in-Publication Data:
Chapman, Anne.
  Herbs.
ISBN 1 875410 64 3.
1. Cookery (Herbs). I. Title. (Series: Country kitchen).
641.657.

CONTENTS

COOKING WITH HERBS

THE HERBS in this book are the herbs I grow most regularly in my garden. I am lucky to live in a warm climate, with plenty of sunlight. Some of the herbs grow in pots; others grow in profusion all over. It is not uncommon for me to find basil beside a rose bush, parsley next to the daisies, and sage by the lavender. I find it a visual delight as I wander around contemplating which herb to put with the roast chicken that night and deciding on the ingredients of a herb soup and a minted banana dessert.

Every herb seems to have a special affinity with a certain food—basil with tomato, mint with lamb, fennel with fish, chives with potatoes, and so on. Herbs enliven familiar dishes and enable you to change the flavour by simply changing the herb. It's fun to substitute herbs and experiment to find you own combination. Mixtures of herbs can vary; indeed, sometimes they have to when certain herbs are not in season.

Flavouring is a very individual art. Eye, taste, intuition and experience determine how to flavour a dish. It is certainly something worth cultivating if you are adventurous. No amount of flavour, however, can disguise bad cooking or poor ingredients. Flavour has to develop along with basic good cooking. The important thing is not what the flavouring is but the harmony of the ingredients complementing the main ingredient. Trust your own palate. Approach food, recipes and flavourings with curiosity and inventiveness. When you are an experienced cook, a recipe will just be an outline from which to create your own dish.

The recipes in this book are for fresh herbs, which are infinitely superior to dried ones. As most herbs are easy to grow in pots as well as in the garden, it's not difficult to have some fresh herbs always at hand. If you must use dried herbs, halve the quantity.

Herbs are used not only in cooking but as medicine. In fact, many began as medicines or oils, essences and perfumes—even love potions. Thyme, bay leaves and rosemary were used in the past as strewing herbs to give a house a clean smell. They are the original disinfectants.

Spices are dried herbs made from the leaves, stalks, roots, seeds, buds, bark or berries of various aromatic plants that nearly always grew only in Asia. The spice trade from Asia to Europe began more than five thousand years ago. Herbs and spices, with their invaluable uses, have been so important to trade that wars have been fought over them.

Storing Herbs

Herbs will keep in the refrigerator for a fortnight if they are fresh. Wash and dry them, and store them in plastic bags or airtight containers.

They can be frozen successfully. Simply choose the freshest leaves, wash them thoroughly, and blanch them by pouring boiling water over them in colander. Dry them in a clean tea towel and seal them in plastic or foil packages in recipe-size quantities. Don't forget to label and date the packages.

The herbs in this garden are so at home and well nourished they have self-seeded between the cracks in the bricks.

Herbs can also be stored dried. The faster they dry the better, so dry them in an oven or microwave. Spread the herbs on a sheet of kitchen paper on a tray and place it in a very low oven overnight. In a microwave oven they will take about five minutes. When cool, put them in screw-top jars and label and seal.

A decorative way of drying herbs is to hang them in bunches. If you live in an area where the air isn't too dirty, simply hang them in a cool, dry position.

BASIL

Provençale chicken cooked in wine with garlic, olives and basil.

ONE OF the great culinary herbs, basil originally came from India and was considered a royal plant. Countries like Greece, Italy and France took it up, and many of their dishes are influenced by its pungent flavour. It is even considered a symbol of fertility in the Mediterranean.

Basil is an annual and is easy to grow. It is a companion plant to tomatoes in the earth and in the kitchen. Tomato and basil perfectly compliment each other.

Basil leaves go well in salads, with cheese and egg dishes, with rice, pasta and pizzas, in soups and stews, and with fish, chicken and lamb. Basil can safely replace coriander and mint in recipes that specify those herbs.

Pesto

Pesto is one of the most wonderful herb dishes ever created. Usually served with pasta, it can also be used to stuff tomatoes, to add flavouring to bean soup, and as a topping to jacket potatoes, split open.

2 cups chopped basil leaves
3 cloves of garlic
3 tablespoons pine nuts
3 tablespoons grated parmesan cheese
3 to 4 tablespoons olive oil
Pepper

Put the basil, garlic and pine nuts into a food processor and blend to a thick paste. Add the parmesan. Now slowly add the olive oil, blending it between the drops. The sauce gradually becomes thick and smooth. Season with pepper.

It can be made the same way with a mortar and pestle.

Pesto can be stored in the refrigerator, with a covering of olive oil.

Guacamole with Basil

A Mexican dish, this is a wonderful starter to a meal as a dip with bread or tortilla chips.

2 large ripe avocados, peeled and mashed
1 green chilli, finely chopped
Juice of half a lemon
Salt and pepper
1 clove of garlic, chopped
2 tablespoons finely chopped basil leaves
Olive oil

Combine the avocadoes, chilli, lemon juice, salt and pepper, garlic and basil and mix well. Pour in a few drops of olive oil until it is smooth and thick.

Rice with Basil and Cheese

A very simple Italian dish of fragrant basil and melted cheese.

1¼ cups arborio rice
2 tablespoons butter, cut up
2 tablespoons finely chopped basil
1 cup grated mozzarella cheese
¼ cup grated parmesan cheese

Bring three cups of water to the boil, add salt to taste, then add the rice. Stir once and put a close-fitting lid on the saucepan. Turn the heat down low and cook for 20 minutes until the rice has absorbed the water.

Put the cooked rice in a warm serving bowl. Fluff it up and mix in the butter and basil. Add the mozzarella and parmesan and mix quickly, as the heat of the rice melts the cheese. Serve immediately.

Provençale Chicken

A magnificent chicken dish from the south of France. Serves 4 to 5.

1.5 kg (3 lb) chicken
2 tablespoons olive oil
2 cups dry white wine
3 cloves of garlic
4 tomatoes, peeled and chopped
2 tablespoons black olives, pitted
2 tablespoons finely chopped basil leaves
Salt and pepper

Cut the chicken into 10 pieces. Heat the oil in a large saucepan and brown the chicken well on all sides. Add the wine, garlic, tomatoes, olives, half the basil, and salt and pepper to taste. Cover and cook simmering for twenty minutes or until tender. Sprinkle the rest of the basil over the chicken and serve.

BAY LEAVES

THE BAY leaf is a culinary herb that can be used successfully fresh or dried. Though not strictly a herb, it is so essential to French and all European cooking that is must be included here. The tree is easy to grow in a sunny place. The leaves are best used two days after they are picked. Throw out the tired old leaves from packages.

The bay tree is a kind of laurel which came originally from Asia. The foliage was used by the ancient Greeks and Romans to make a 'crown of laurels', a symbol of wisdom and glory.

The sweet, resinous smell of bay leaf will enhance any marinade, stock, soup or stew, boiled meats and terrines, fish, vegetable and rice dishes, as well as flavouring ice-creams and custards.

Roast Pork with Bay Leaves

A succulent pork dish penetrated with the aromatic flavour of bay leaves. The skin of the pork is removed for this dish. Serves 6.

1½ tablespoons butter
1½ tablespoons olive oil
1 kg (2 lb) pork loin, boned and tied
Salt and pepper
10 bay leaves
¼ cup red wine vinegar
1 cup white wine

Put the butter and oil together in a heavy pot just large enough to contain the meat. Brown the meat well on all sides, then add salt and pepper to taste, the bay leaves, vinegar and water. Bring to the boil, stirring the liquid, then turn the heat down very low, cover tightly and cook for about two hours or until the pork is very tender. Check occasionally in case the liquid is drying up — add a little water if necessary.

Put the pork on a warm platter, surrounded by the bay leaves. Remove the fat from the sauce, then bring the remaining juice to the boil, adding a little more wine if there isn't enough juice. Spoon the sauce over the pork and serve.

Fish Kebabs

The bay leaves protect the fish and add their oil to the flavour of the fish. Serves 4.

4 whiting fillets (or similar)
Bay leaves
Salt and pepper
Juice of 1 lemon
1½ tablespoons olive oil

Cut the whiting into large bite-size pieces. Put them on 4 skewers, alternating the fish with the bay leaves. Sprinkle salt and pepper, lemon juice and olive oil over them in a gratin dish. Marinate until time to grill them over hot coals. Baste with the left-over marinade.

Roast pork with bay leaves is an aromatic dish. Cooked this way, the pork is tender and succulent and subtle of flavour. Serve the meat juices with the fat removed.

10

Barbecued Steak

The small end of rump steak is the sweetest and tastiest piece of steak for grilling. Cook in one piece and then slice to serve when done.

1 large slice of rump steak, 4 cm (1½ in.)
  thick
1 tablespoon olive oil
1 tablespoon crushed peppercorns
Fresh bay leaves
Salt

Put the steak in a dish and pour the oil and pepper over it. Let it marinate for several hours. Turn once.

When the coals for the barbecue are ready, put a layer of bay leaves on the top of the rump and turn it over as it is placed on the grill so that the bay leaves protect the steak from the fire. Now put a layer of leaves on the top of the steak. Seal both sides of the meat for two minutes each and then turn again twice only. When the surface is firm and the meat springs back when touched, it is done.

Put on a warm platter and let stand for 15 minutes to relax the muscles of the meat. Remove the bay leaves and slice the steak crossways. Serve with the meat juices and Dijon mustard.

VARIATION: The steak is nearly as tasty cooked on a ridged skillet on the stove. Cook exactly the same way.

CHERVIL

CHERVIL IS a small biennial herb with a delicate fern-like leaf. It originated in southern Russia and the Middle East and is now native all over Europe. It grows to about 45 cm (18 in.) high and should be pruned to encourage growth. It likes moisture and semi-shade.

Chervil tastes a little like parsley, but more delicate, and slightly like anise. It is one of the most important herbs in French cooking. It is a usual herb in *fines herbes*. Chervil is best used at the end of cooking. It is wonderful with all egg dishes, fish and shellfish, meats, salads, sauces and vegetables.

Chervil Soup

This old country-style soup from Belgium brings out the delicate flavour of chervil. Serves 4 to 6.

1 tablespoon butter
1 cup peeled and diced potato
1 leek, sliced
1 small onion, sliced
5 cups chicken stock
1 tablespoon cornflour
2 tablespoons milk
Salt and pepper
1½ tablespoons finely chopped chervil

Melt the butter in a saucepan and add the potato, leek and onion. Cook, stirring gently, until the onion is soft. Add the stock and simmer for 30 minutes.

Put the mixture through a food processor and return to the saucepan. Put on low heat. Mix the cornflour with the milk and add to the soup to thicken it. Add salt and pepper to taste.

Just before serving, add the chervil.

Grilled Veal Chops

A simple but elegant dish. Serve with waxy potatoes and a green salad. Serves 4.

4 veal chops
Salt and pepper
1½ tablespoons butter
1 tablespoon chervil

Sprinkle pepper on the chops and grill them for 3 minutes each side or until cooked to your taste. Salt to taste when cooked.

Mix the butter and chervil to a smooth paste. Place the veal chops on a warm platter, dot with the chervil butter and serve.

VARIATION: The chervil butter is just as delicious with grilled lamb chops.

Lamb with Herb Crust

Serves 2 to 3.

1 rack of lamb, trimmed of fat
1 cup breadcrumbs
½ cup finely chopped chervil
1 clove of garlic, finely chopped
2 tablespoons Dijon mustard
1 tablespoon olive oil
Salt and pepper to taste

Preheat the oven to 200°C (400°F). Combine the breadcrumbs, chervil, garlic, mustard, oil, salt and pepper. Coat both sides of the rack of lamb with the mixture; it will form a crust to seal the meat. Place the lamb on a grilling rack in a roasting pan and put it in the oven. It should be ready in 20 to 30 minutes depending on how pink you like it.

CHIVES

CHIVES BELONG to the onion family but have a much more delicate flavour. They grow easily in the sun and need moisture and top dressing twice a year. Cut them off with scissors.

Chives are an ideal garnish, particularly for egg dishes, cottage and cream cheeses, sprinkled on soups, potatoes, carrots and salads.

Potato Salad

Waxy potatoes are best for this salad, as they will hold their shape and absorb the dressing.

1 kg (2 lb) waxy potatoes
1 tablespoon white wine vinegar
3 tablespoons olive oil
1 tablespoon Dijon mustard
Salt and pepper
2 onions, chopped
2 tablespoons chopped chives

Boil or steam the potatoes until they are slightly underdone. Peel them immediately and cut into thick slices. Mix together the vinegar, oil, mustard, salt and pepper. Pour this mixture over the potatoes, along with the onions and half the chives, while the potatoes are still warm. Sprinkle the rest of the chives on when serving.

Chive Cream Cheese

This is an excellent dip to serve with water biscuits or crusty herbed bread.

1 cup cottage cheese
1 cup yoghurt
1½ tablespoons finely chopped chives
1 clove of garlic, finely chopped
Pepper

Blend the cottage cheese and the yoghurt in a blender. Mix all the ingredients together well and refrigerate until serving.

The chives in the foreground of this picture have just finished flowering and scattering their seeds for new growth.

Scrambled Eggs

4 eggs
1 tablespoon chopped chives
Salt and pepper
30 g (1 oz) butter

Break the eggs into a bowl and mix, but not too much. Add the chives, salt and pepper. Heat the butter in a saucepan and pour in the egg mixture. Let it sit, just tilting the pan now and then. As the eggs thicken and while still runny, remove from heat and gently scramble with a wooden spoon. They are ready when they are still a bit runny. Serve immediately.

CORIANDER

CORIANDER IS a hardy annual and is grown for its bright green leaves and its seed. Coriander has been used in cooking and medicine for thousands of years. It is mentioned in the Old Testament and recorded in India and China. It is sometimes called 'Chinese parsley'.

Green coriander is one of the most commonly used herbs in Asia, the Middle East and South America. It is the basis of many curries, spicy sauces, fresh chutneys and salads.

Coriander and Rice Soup

The fresh herbs and the spices harmonise well in this soup from India. Serves 4.

1 tablespoon oil
1 tablespoon chopped spring onions
1 teaspoon finely chopped ginger
1 teaspoon ground coriander seeds
1 teaspoon ground cumin seeds
6 cups chicken stock
Juice of half a lemon
1 red chilli
Salt and pepper
1 cup long-grain rice, washed
1 tablespoon flour
1 cup yoghurt
3 tablespoons coriander leaves

Heat the oil in a saucepan and add the spring onions, ginger, coriander and cumin. Stir for a few minutes and then add the chicken stock, lemon juice, chilli, salt and pepper. Bring to the boil and add the rice. Cover the saucepan and simmer for 20 minutes.

When the rice is cooked, mix the flour and yoghurt together and gradually add to the soup. It will thicken up. Do not boil. The flour prevents the yoghurt from curdling. Stir for 5 minutes and serve with the coriander leaves strewn on top.

Corn Bread with Coriander

This is a soda bread and very simple and fast to make. It is delicious eaten warm.

2 corn cobs
2 cups wholemeal flour
2 cups flour
2 teaspoons salt
2 teaspoons sugar
1 teaspoon bicarbonate of soda
¾ teaspoon baking powder
1 tablespoon butter
⅓ cup finely chopped coriander leaves
1½ cups buttermilk

Take the husks and silk off the corn cobs and slice off the kernels. Strain the juice from the kernels by pressing hard in a sieve.

Sift the flours, salt, sugar, soda and baking powder into a large bowl. Rub the butter in until the mixture resembles breadcrumbs. Stir in the coriander and then the buttermilk and mix to a soft dough.

Place on a greased baking tray and, with floured hands, form into a 20 cm (8 in.) round. Use a sharp, floured knife to cut a 1 cm (½ in.) deep cross in the top of the dough. Bake in an oven preheated to 190°C (375°F) for 45 minutes or until the loaf sounds hollow when tapped on the bottom.

Coriander chicken is a very simple spicy dish to make if you have previously prepared the garam masala.

Coriander Chicken

This spicy chicken is cooked on a bed of coriander and yoghurt. It is simply delicious. I include a recipe for garam masala, as it is superior to the bought ones. It will keep up to six months in an airtight bottle in the refrigerator. Serves 4 to 5.

1 chicken (free range if possible)
2 onions, chopped
2 cups chopped fresh coriander
4 cloves of garlic
1 tablespoon chopped fresh ginger
½ tablespoon olive oil
Juice of half a lemon
1 teaspoon turmeric
Salt
4 red chillies
1 cup yoghurt
2 tomatoes, peeled and chopped

Garam masala
4 tablespoons coriander seeds
1 tablespoon black peppercorns
3 tablespoons cumin seeds
1 tablespoon cardamom pods
4 cinnamon sticks
1 teaspoon cloves
1 nutmeg, finely grated

Make the garam masala first. Dry roast all the seeds except the nutmeg in a small pan. Roast the spices one at a time. When their fragrance is released, they are roasted. Take the seeds out of the cardamom pods. Blend all the seeds to a powder. Add the nutmeg and mix well.

Cut the chicken into 10 pieces. Take off all the fat and the skin. Into the food processor put the onions, coriander, garlic and ginger. Blend to a pulp.

Heat the oil in a large saucepan and put in the herb mixture. Stir for a minute or two, then add the lemon juice, turmeric, garam masala, salt, red chillies, yoghurt and tomatoes. Stir for another five minutes, then add the chicken pieces. Coat them with the herb mixture and stir for a few minutes. Turn down the heat, put a tight-fitting lid on the saucepan and simmer for an hour.

VARIATION: Lamb is just as nice in this herb sauce. Cut it into bite-size pieces. Serve with spicy yellow rice and a yoghurt salad.

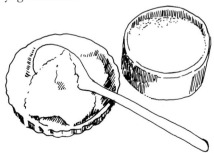

DILL

DILL IS grown for its seeds and its leaves. Although it originated in southern Europe, it heavily influenced Scandinavian, German, Russian and Balkan cooking. It is an annual and easy to grow from seed.

Dill has a delicate flavour resembling caraway. It transforms cucumbers into the popular dill pickles. It is especially good with fish, cream cheese, potatoes and carrots and as a garnish for casseroles.

Grilled Trout with Dill Butter

The dill and Pernod in this dish make it absolutely delicious. Remember to put in extra salt, because trout is a freshwater fish. Serves 4.

4 whole small trout, cleaned
1 cup finely chopped dill
1 cup finely chopped parsley
Zest of 1 lemon
2 teaspoons salt
Pepper
2 tablespoons oil

For the dill butter
2 tablespoons wine vinegar
3 tablespoons Pernod
2¼ tablespoons butter, cut into small pieces
3 tablespoons chopped dill

Clean and pat the trout dry with kitchen paper. Combine the dill, parsley, lemon zest, salt and pepper. Stuff the trout with the herb mixture. Sew up the fish or fasten with a steel skewer. Brush with the oil.

To make the butter, put the vinegar

on the stove and boil for a few minutes, remove from heat and add the Pernod. Now add the butter, piece by piece, stirring all the time. Add the dill.

Put the trout under a grill, turn a few times while cooking, basting with the oil. They should be ready in about 15 to 20 minutes. Trout are better undercooked than overcooked. Split the trout open and pour the dill butter over the flesh. Serve with boiled waxy potatoes.

Cottage Cheese and Dill Dip

2 cups cottage cheese
1 tablespoon yoghurt
2 tablespoons finely chopped dill
2 spring onions, finely chopped
Pepper

Blend the cottage cheese with the yoghurt in a food processor until smooth. Mix all the ingredients well together. Refrigerate until serving.

Carrots with Dill

Carrots and dill go particularly well together. The addition of the spices makes a special dish to accompany blander food such as chops or grilled chicken. Serves 4.

2 tablespoons vegetable oil
$\frac{1}{2}$ teaspoon cumin seeds
1 tablespoon finely chopped fresh ginger
2 green chillies
2 cups chopped carrots
1 teaspoon coriander seeds, ground
1 teaspoon turmeric

1 cup chopped dill
Salt and pepper

Heat the oil in a pan and put in the cumin seeds and then the ginger and chillies. Keep stirring for a few minutes and then add the carrots, coriander and turmeric. Stir for a minute and add the dill, salt and pepper. Stir again, reduce the heat and cover, simmering until the carrots are done. Remove the carrots with a slotted spoon.

Cucumber Soup

A nice chilled soup for a hot summer day. Serves 6.

4 cups peeled and chopped cucumber
1 onion, chopped
3 cups chicken stock
A bouquet garni (page 44) including dill and lemon peel
Salt and pepper
1 cup yoghurt or sour cream
1 cup chopped dill
2 spring onions, finely chopped

Put 2 cups of cucumber and the onion in the saucepan with the chicken stock, bouquet garni, salt and pepper. Bring to the boil and simmer for 15 minutes. Remove the bouquet garni and blend the soup in a food processor.

Put the soup in a soup tureen and let it cool. Put the rest of the cucumber and the yoghurt or sour cream in the food processor and blend until smooth. Add this to the soup and stir in the dill and spring onions. Refrigerate until ready to serve.

FENNEL

FENNEL IS a tall, hardy perennial which grows wild in temperate climates. The fresh fronds are used as a herb, the seeds are aromatic and used to flavour pickles, biscuits and fish, and the stalks of fennel are dried and used as a base to cook on. Florence fennel is grown for its bulb, which is used as a vegetable and salad.

Fennel tastes strongly of anise. The fronds or leaves are an accompaniment to fish and pork, either as a sauce or to cook with it. Finely chopped, it is used as a garnish to soups, salads and casseroles.

Fennel Chicken

This is a country-style chicken dish from Italy. The fennel flavours the chicken in a most subtle and delicious way.

10 fennel stalks
6 bay leaves
1 large free-range chicken
3 cloves of garlic
A strip of lemon peel
125 g (4 oz) pancetta (or bacon), finely chopped
Pepper

2 tablespoon butter, cut into small pieces
3 tablespoons brandy

Line the bottom of the pot in which you will bake the chicken with the fennel stalks and bay leaves. Clean and pat dry the chicken and stuff it with the garlic, lemon, pancetta and some pepper. Lay the chicken on its side on top of the herbs in the pot. Sprinkle the butter over it and grind some more pepper over the outside of the chicken. Cover and put in an oven preheated to 200°C (400°F).

Cook for 30 minutes and then turn the chicken on its other side, basting with the butter. Cook a further 30 minutes and then turn the chicken breast-upwards. Cook uncovered for another 15 minutes or until it is cooked and golden brown. Remove from the oven and put on a low heat on the stove.

Warm the brandy, ignite, and quickly and carefully pour it over the fennel and chicken. When the flames have died down, transfer the fennel stalks and bay leaves with the chicken on top to a warm serving dish.

Take the fat off the meat juices. Cook the liquid for another 3 or 4 minutes, stirring all the while. Serve this sauce separately. Serve the pancetta pieces with the chicken.

19

Fish Flamed in Fennel

A whole fish is grilled over a bed of
fennel sticks, then ignited.

1 large whole fish, gutted and cleaned
Juice and peel of 1 lemon
Dry fennel sticks
Salt and pepper
2 tablespoons olive oil

Pat dry the fish. Stuff the lemon peel
and a stick of fennel into the fish.
Marinate the fish with salt and pepper,
oil and lemon juice.

Lay the fennel sticks in a shallow
flameproof dish. Lay the fish over the
fennel and pour half the marinade
over it. Put under the grill for seven
minutes, then turn, marinate and grill
the other side for ten minutes or until
cooked.

Take from under the grill. Set the
fennel alight. The smoky fennel flavour
enhances the fish flavour very subtly.

Carrot Salad

Choose the fine new shoots of the
fennel for this wonderful, simple salad.

2 tablespoons finely chopped new fennel leaves
2 tablespoons olive oil
1 teaspoon lemon juice
1 teaspoon Dijon mustard
Salt and pepper
500 g (1 lb) carrots

Combine the fennel, oil, lemon juice,
mustard, salt and pepper in a screw-top
jar and shake well. Grate the carrots,
then pour the vinaigrette over them,
mixing gently. Refrigerate until serving.

The barbecue is perfect for cooking fish flamed in
fennel.

GARLIC

GARLIC BELONGS to the same family
as the onion and it is just as highly
regarded. It is used every day in
cooking all over Europe, the Middle
East, Asia and South America. In a
moderate climate it can be grown from
a bulb.

Garlic is extremely good for you.
It aids digestion, it is an antiseptic,
it reduces blood pressure, lowers
cholestrol and clears bronchitis. Garlic
can make the dullest dish interesting.
Cooked garlic is not as strongly
flavoured as raw garlic and can be
safely eaten. Chew parsley to neutralise
garlic breath. Press on the garlic cloves
with a broad knife to release the
aroma and make it easy to peel.

To list all the ways to use garlic
would be impossible. It is essential in
curries and chutneys and will enhance
most savoury dishes.

Garlic Lamb

This is an old French peasant way of
cooking lamb. It takes a long time to
cook so slowly but is well worth the
effort—the meat is so tender, a knife is
hardly needed to cut it. Serve with
lentils and brussels sprouts. Serves 8.

1 leg of lamb
1 tablespoon butter
1 tablespoon olive oil
2 teaspoons sugar
1 cup white wine
1 cup hot water
Pepper and salt
6 small onions, peeled
3 carrots, sliced
6 cloves of garlic
A bouquet garni (page 44)

Trim the fat off the lamb. Heat the butter and oil in a heavy pan. Brown the leg on all sides, then add the sugar, wine and water. Season with pepper. Add the whole onions, carrots, garlic, bouquet garni and salt. Lower the heat, cover, and simmer for 5 hours, turning the meat over a few times.

Transfer the meat and onions to a warm platter. Strain and remove the fat from the liquid. Reduce the sauce by half. Pour a little over the lamb and serve the rest separately.

Garlic Soup

Don't be frightened off by the large quantity of garlic. Cooked this way it loses its pungency and becomes surprisingly mild. This is a rich country soup from the south-west of France. Serves 6.

2 cups chicken stock
6 cups water
A bouquet garni (page 44)
2 tablespoons goose fat or butter
24 cloves of garlic, peeled
Salt and pepper
1 teaspoon grated nutmeg
3 eggs, yolks and whites separated
6 slices stale bread
2 tablespoons olive oil

Bring the stock, water, and bouquet garni to the boil. Remove from heat. Melt the goose fat or butter in a saucepan and add the garlic cloves. Cook gently, and just before they brown pour the stock over them. Add the salt, pepper and nutmeg and cook for 15 minutes. Blend in a food processor and return to the saucepan.

Spread the eggwhites on the slices of bread and toast in the oven.

Beat the egg yolks and olive oil together. Add a little soup to the egg mixture, then gradually pour the mixture into the soup, stirring all the time. Do not let it boil again.

To serve, put a slice of bread in each soup bowl and ladle over the garlic soup.

Chicken with Garlic

I first ate this dish in Thailand. It was so delicious I have attempted to emulate it here. Cooked on a barbecue, it is even nicer. Serve with rice or baked kumera.

1 large free-range chicken
10 cloves of garlic
1 teaspoon salt
2 tablespoons coconut cream
1 red chilli, chopped
1 tablespoon pepper
1 cup chopped fresh coriander
1 cup chopped fresh mint
Juice of 1 lemon

Cut the chicken into 10 pieces. Mix all the other ingredients together to make the marinade. Rub the marinade into the chicken and let it marinate for 12 hours if possible.

Grill the chicken pieces on a grill tray under a very hot grill. Turn every 5 minutes until the chicken is tender.

Garlic soup is a real country style dish, and surprisingly subtle.

Overleaf: I gathered and composed this nasturtium and mint salad one Sunday morning while wandering around a country garden. Feel free to use your imagination with salad combinations.

MARJORAM

MARJORAM IS a perennial and, in warm countries, is very easy to grow. It has a delicate perfume, so it is wise to add it just before the end of cooking. An extremely versatile herb, marjoram can be used for every dish you would use thyme for. The two herbs go very well together, too. Oregano (page 29) is the wild variety.

Marjoram is a favourite herb for poultry stuffings; it makes delicious sandwiches with cream cheese; it goes well with salads, omelettes, sauces, vinegars, pizzas, meat loaves and sausages and with poultry, pork and veal.

My version of the northern European dish mock hare. Albrecht Dürer's classic study of a hare is in the background.

Crumbed Green Beans

A dear friend cooks her beans this way. They are deliciously crunchy.

500 g (1 lb) green beans
1 tablespoon butter
3 tablespoons soft white breadcrumbs
1 tablespoon marjoram

Trim the tops off the beans and otherwise leave whole. Cook in boiling water for about 10 minutes; they should be still a bit crisp and not soft. Drain.

Heat the butter in the saucepan and stir in the breadcrumbs; keep stirring until they are almost golden. Put the beans back in along with the marjoram. Stir for about a minute or two to warm the beans, and serve.

Mock Hare

A traditional Sunday dish from the north of Germany. It is often shaped into the form of a sleeping hare. It's fun to shape, and it gives the meat loaf more interest. Use your cat as a model, remembering to change the ears. Shape as a egg first, the smaller end being the head.

500 g (1 lb) lean mince beef
500 g (1 lb) lean mince pork
4 eggs, beaten
2 onions, finely chopped
1 leek, finely chopped
2 cups breadcrumbs
2 tablespoons marjoram
3 juniper berries, crushed
Salt and pepper
1 teaspoon paprika

Combine all the ingredients in a bowl and mix thoroughly.

Attempt to shape your hare. If you give up, you can just mould it into a long roll. Place onto a greased tray and cook in a preheated oven at 180°C (350°F) for about 1 hour. It is cooked when the outside is golden brown and, when skewered, red meat juices do not flow.

Serve with gravy made with the meat juices that will flow out of the meat, a little flour, wine and water. Mashed potatoes and parsnips go well with mock hare.

Onion and Olive Pizza

Pizzas can be made with all sorts of combinations of toppings. This one is very simple and fast. It is more like pizzas would have been made a hundred years ago, as it is made in a pan on top of the stove. It has a firm, crunchy texture rather like a biscuit. There isn't any yeast in the dough. This pizza is 18 cm (7 in.) across. Serves 4 for a starter, 2 for a main meal.

125 g (4 oz) flour
1 teaspoon salt
1 teaspoon baking powder
3 tablespoons water
3 tablespoons olive oil
4 onions, finely sliced
15 black olives, stoned and halved
1 tablespoon marjoram
Salt and pepper

Sieve the flour, salt and baking powder in a mound on a board. Make a well and put in 2 tablespoons of cold water. Make it into a dough, adding a little water when necessary. Knead it for a few minutes, then roll it out in a round about 18 cm (7 in.) in diameter.

Heat half the olive oil in a pan and add the onions. Cook until soft and golden. Remove from heat.

Heat the rest of the oil in a heavy pan and when very hot put the round of dough in. Adjust the oil so that it comes just to the top of the dough. Cook for 5 minutes on a medium heat; when the underside is golden, turn it over.

Now, very quickly spread the onion slices over the crust, place the olives in circles on it, and scatter the marjoram evenly. Season with salt and pepper. Cover the pan and cook for another 5 minutes or until it is ready. Serve immediately.

MINT

MINT HAS a very fresh, clean taste and perfume. Mints are perennial, but their foliage dies away in winter. They are grown by propagation and need rich soil, plenty of water and partial shade. There are many varieties from Asia as well as Europe, but the most common varieties for culinary use are round-leaved mints, which include apple mint, spearmint and bergamot mint.

Mints have traditionally been used as a medicine to cure all sorts of diseases. In Asia, the Middle East and England, mint is one of the most common herbs. It makes a wonderful salad herb. Lamb marries happily with mint, as do mince dishes. Mint can be used with fruit such as oranges, bananas and pineapples. It goes well with carrots, potatoes, peas and beans, lentils, tomatoes and eggplant (aubergine). In Asia it is used in curries, fresh salads and chutneys.

Shape the meat mixture into smooth balls. Heat the oil and fry the meat balls a few at a time until they are brown all over. Keep them warm in a hot serving dish. Serve with hot potato salad, coleslaw and a jar of pickles.

Minty Meat Balls

Delicious meat balls from Albania. Mint is almost the national flavour, it is so popular. Serves 4.

500 g (1 lb) lamb, minced
2 eggs, beaten
2 cloves of garlic, crushed
3 tablespoons finely chopped mint
1 teaspoon cinnamon
¼ teaspoon cayenne
Salt and pepper
½ cup olive oil

Combine all the ingredients except the oil in a mixing bowl and knead until smooth. Leave for two hours, covered, in the refrigerator.

Pineapple and Mint

1 pineapple
2 tablespoons finely chopped mint
3 tablespoons castor sugar
Juice of 2 oranges
2 tablespoons kirsch

Peel and cut the pineapple into small pieces. Do this over a bowl, so you don't lose the juice. Strain the juice into a saucepan with the mint, sugar and orange juice. Bring to the boil and simmer for a few minutes. Add the kirsch when it cools down. Pour the liquid over the pineapple pieces. Refrigerate. Serve sprinkled with sprigs of fresh mint.

Catmint is definitely easier to grow than to find in the shops. It is well worth growing a pot or two.

Nasturtium and Mint Salad

Tiny spinach leaves
Tiny cos lettuce leaves
1 cucumber, sliced
1 carrot, sliced
Tom Thumb tomatoes
Apple mint leaves, whole
Nasturtium flowers and leaves
Violets

Vinaigrette
3 tablespoons olive oil
Juice of half a lemon
1 clove of garlic, squashed
Salt and pepper

Arrange all the salad ingredients attractively in a salad bowl. Put the vinaigrette ingredients in a screw-top jar and shake until mixed. Dress the salad at the table.

OREGANO

OREGANO IS the wild variety of marjoram and has a much more pungent and powerful flavour. It is easy to grow in well-drained soil and a sunny position.

Oregano is very important in Italian and Greek cooking and is excellent with tomatoes, cheese, beans, zucchini (courgettes), eggplant (aubergine), fish, beef, mince dishes and pizzas.

Spaghetti alla Rustica

Serves 4.

3 tablespoons olive oil
2 cloves of garlic, crushed and chopped
2 tablespoons rinsed and chopped anchovy
*   fillets*
2 tablespoons finely chopped oregano
500 g (1 lb) spaghetti
2 tablespoons finely chopped parsley
Pepper
Parmesan cheese, freshly grated

Heat the oil in a pan and put in the garlic and anchovies. Stir them into a mash and add the oregano. Remove from heat.

Meanwhile, cook the spaghetti in a large pan of boiling water. Drain and put into a warm bowl. Add the anchovy mixture, the parsley and pepper. Stir and serve immediately with a bowl of parmesan.

Barbecued Oregano Prawns

Keeping the shells and heads on may seem a little fiddly, but prawns retain the most flavour if they are kept in their shell, and the flavour is absolutely worth it. Serves 4 to 6.

1 kg (2 lb) green prawns
½ cup vegetable oil
Pepper
1 tablespoon finely chopped oregano
Juice of 1 lemon
2 spring onions, finely chopped
6 spring onions cut in 2.5 cm (1 in.) lengths
Fresh sprigs of oregano

Prepare the prawns by running a sharp knife along the back to pierce the shell and flesh, then de-vein them and wash thoroughly, but keep the head on and the shell almost intact.

Mix together the marinade of oil, pepper, oregano, lemon juice and chopped spring onions. Put the prepared prawns into the marinade, making sure some gets inside the shells. Marinate for at least 2 hours.

Thread the prawns onto skewers, alternating with spring onions and sprigs of oregano. Put them on the barbecue for 5 to 10 minutes depending on their size, turning several times and brushing with marinade.

VARIATION: This dish can be made just as simply under the griller or stir-fried in a wok with chilli-flavoured oil.

Mushrooms Oregano

A simply made dish which can be eaten hot or cold as a salad or as an accompaniment to meat dishes.

2 tablespoons olive oil
500 g (1 lb) small button mushrooms
2 teaspoons salt
2 cloves of garlic, chopped
1 tablespoon fresh oregano
Juice of half a lemon
Pepper

Heat the oil in a pan and add the mushrooms. Cook for a minute, then add the salt. Cook, stirring, for five minutes then add the garlic, oregano, lemon juice and pepper. Mix well. Remove from the heat as soon as the mushrooms soften.

PARSLEY

PARSLEY IS the most widely known of herbs all over the world. It has been used for thousands of years as a medicine as well as a flavouring. It is a biennial and easy to grow in fairly rich soil and a sunny position. The most common varieties are the curly-leaved and the flat-leaved, known as Italian parsley.

It is packed with vitamins A,B and C and is used as a general tonic. As a culinary herb it is indispensible for bouquet garni and *fines herbes*; it adds flavour to mashed potatoes, salads, eggs, sandwiches, stuffings, vegetables and sauces—in fact, almost all savoury dishes.

Oregano and chives are flourishing in these beautiful terracotta pots against a background of flowering rosemary.

Tabbouleh Salad

This delicious, pungent salad of parsley and mint is traditionally served in individual bowls with lettuce leaves or vine leaves to scoop the salad up with.

1 cup fine burghul (cracked wheat)
3 tablespoons finely chopped spring onions
1½ cups finely chopped parsley
½ cup finely chopped mint
1 tomato, peeled and finely chopped
3 tablespoons olive oil
1 tablespoon lemon juice
Salt and pepper
Lettuce or vine leaves

First soak the burghul in water for half an hour. Drain and dry.

Combine the burghul, spring onions, parsley, mint, tomato, oil and lemon juice. Add salt and pepper to taste. Serve with the leaves.

VARIATION: Decorate with black olives.

31

Green Sauce

This French sauce is excellent for serving with any meat or fish dish, hot or cold. Make it just before serving.

1 egg yolk
1 tablespoon Dijon mustard
1 cup olive oil
2 tablespoons lemon juice
Salt and pepper
2 tablespoons freshly chopped parsley
1 tablespoon freshly chopped tarragon
1 tablespoon freshly chopped chives
1 tablespoon freshly chopped chervil

Put the egg yolk in a bowl along with the mustard. Mix and gradually add the oil drop by drop as you do when making mayonnaise. Stir in the lemon juice at the end and add pepper and salt and the parsley, tarragon, chives and chervil. Serve.

Barley Soup with Parsley

A really old-fashioned hearty soup. The lamb adds a sweet taste. Serves 6 to 8.

½ cup split peas
2 onions, chopped
A bouquet garni (page 44)
1 cup barley
A piece of neck of lamb, trimmed of fat
9 cups water
Salt and pepper
3 carrots, chopped
1 swede, chopped
3 parsnips, chopped
1 cup chopped parsley
3 tablespoons chopped parsley

Put the split peas in a bowl and pour boiling water over them. Let stand for an hour and the peas will soften. Drain.

Into a large saucepan put the peas, onions, bouquet garni, barley, lamb, water, salt and pepper. Bring to the boil, cover and simmer for an hour. Add the carrots, swede, parsnips and cup of parsley and simmer 45 to 60 minutes until all the vegetables are soft. Serve with the extra parsley sprinkled on top.

Parsleyed Ham (Jambon Persillé)

2 cups chicken stock
2 cups dry white wine
1.5 kg (3 lb) cooked ham
Pepper
4 juniper berries, crushed
2½ tablespoons gelatine
1 cup finely chopped parsley
2 tablespoons white wine vinegar

Put the stock and wine into a saucepan and bring to the boil. Add the ham, some pepper and the juniper berries and simmer for half an hour or until the ham is tender.

Take the ham out and reserve the hot liquid. Either cut the ham into bite-size pieces or flake it, pulling it apart with your fingers. Put the pieces into a bowl or a terrine dish.

Soften the gelatine in a little cold water and then stir into the hot liquid. When it is dissolved, allow the liquid to cool. Add the parsley and vinegar and pour over the ham. Let it set in the refrigerator.

To serve, unmould from the bowl or serve it in the terrine dish.

*An old country dish, parsleyed ham (*jambon persillé*) is a refreshing meat dish for a special-occasion summer lunch.*

32

ROSEMARY

Spring lamb with rosemary is a special dish to cook for a celebratory lunch or dinner.

ROSEMARY IS a very hardy evergreen bush with pale blue flowers and spiky leaves. It is very aromatic and smells something like pine needles. It will grow in any warm place. It is the herb of remembrance which Australia and New Zealand soldiers wear on Anzac Day to remember their fallen comrades. Rosemary grows wild in Turkey and the Mediterranean. It has many medicinal virtues.

Rosemary has a great affinity with lamb, pork and chicken. It is excellent in soups and stews, with tomatoes and vegetables. It is one of the few herbs that go well with sweet dishes such as ice-cream, sorbets, cakes, puddings and creams.

Rosemary Turnips

Serve these aromatic turnips with chicken or duck and mashed potatoes.

6 small white turnips
1½ tablespoons butter
2 cloves of garlic, crushed
3 sprigs of rosemary

Slice the turnips. Cook them for five minutes in boiling water or until half-cooked. Drain.

Melt the butter in a pan and put in the turnip slices, garlic and rosemary. Keep turning them so they cook evenly. They will go a golden colour.

Spring Lamb with Rosemary

2 tablespoons olive oil
1 tablespoon butter
A small leg of lamb, trimmed of fat
3 cloves of garlic, crushed
6 sprigs of rosemary about 8 cm (3 in.) long
Salt and pepper
2 cups dry white wine

Heat the oil and butter in a large saucepan. Add the lamb, garlic and rosemary. Brown the lamb well on all sides. Add salt and pepper and 1½ cups of the white wine. Bring to the boil, cover and simmer for 1½ to 2 hours until the lamb is very tender. Turn two or three times during cooking.

Transfer the lamb, sitting on the sprigs of rosemary, to a warm serving plate. Take the fat off the cooking liquid and add the rest of the wine and water if necessary. Boil very fast for a few minutes, stirring all the while. Serve the sauce separately.

Pork and Veal Pâté

There are all sorts of variations to pâtés and terrines. It is fun to experiment with the herbs and spices.

250 g (8 oz) bacon
750 g (1½ lb) pork, minced
500 g (1 lb) veal, minced
1 onion, finely chopped
Salt and pepper
1 teaspoon grated nutmeg
2 tablespoons chopped rosemary
2 tablespoons chopped parsley
2 cloves of garlic, chopped

Take the rind off the bacon and line a terrine dish or loaf tin with it. Mix together half the pork, the veal, the onion, salt and pepper, and nutmeg. Then mix the remaining pork with the herbs, garlic and some salt and pepper.

Put half the pork and veal mixture into the terrine in a smooth layer, then add the pork and herb mixture. Finally add the remaining pork and veal mince.

Cover the terrine with foil and put in a roasting pan with water. Place in a preheated oven at 180°C (360°F) for 1¼ hours. Remove from the oven and place a weight on top of the terrine until it is cold. Turn out and refrigerate until serving.

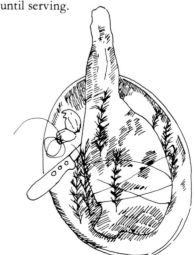

SAGE

SAGE IS another medicinal herb now used as flavouring. The sage bush will grow for years in a sunny, well-drained position. The flavour of sage is very powerful, so care should be taken not to use too much.

It is an excellent herb to use with rich dishes like duck, goose, rabbit, pork or sausages. The Italians love it with veal and calf's liver. It is incomparably better fresh than dried.

Rabbit with Prunes

This homely dish is usually served with potatoes and brussels sprouts or red cabbage. Serves 4.

1 tablespoon olive oil
1 tablespoon butter
1 rabbit, cut in pieces
1 onion, sliced
1 carrot, sliced
2 cloves of garlic
3 cups red wine
1 teaspoon sage
A bouquet garni (page 44)
3 juniper berries
Salt and pepper
30 prunes, pitted and soaked

Melt the oil and butter in a pan and brown the rabbit pieces. Add the onion and carrot. Let it sweat a little, stir, then add the garlic, red wine, sage and bouquet garni. Bring to the boil and add the juniper berries and salt and pepper to taste. Cover and simmer for an hour and a quarter or until tender.

Add the prunes for the last fifteen minutes of cooking. If the sauce is very thin, drain off the liquid and reduce by boiling very fast to a thick consistency.

Potato Purée

A delicious sage purée to serve with pork or sausages. Nice enough a dish on its own.

1 kg (2 lb) potatoes
1½ teaspoons olive oil
1 onion, chopped
2 cups stock
¼ teaspoon chopped sage
Salt and pepper
2 tablespoons butter

Peel the potatoes and boil them until tender.

Put the oil in a pan and when hot add the onion. Sauté until transparent. Add the stock, sage, salt and pepper and boil down to one-third of the volume.

Mash the potatoes thoroughly and mix with the sage bouillon and the butter over a moderate heat. Mix to a smooth purée. Serve.

Sage Biscuits

Crisp, crunchy biscuits with the delightful combination of sage and cheddar. They are great to hand around with pre-lunch drinks.

2 cups flour
1 tablespoon baking powder
2 tablespoons butter, cut into sticks
½ cup grated cheddar cheese
2 tablespoons finely chopped sage
¼ teaspoon cayenne
¾ cup milk

Sift the flour and baking powder into a large bowl. Put the butter and cheese into the flour and blend until it resembles breadcrumbs. Add the sage

Sage biscuits are quick and easy to make and a great favourite with my family.

and cayenne. Stir in some of the milk and mix, adding more milk as needed. Knead the dough lightly on a floured board and roll out to 6 mm ($\frac{1}{4}$ in.) thick. Cut into rounds and place on a baking tray, separated from each other. Bake in an oven preheated to 215°C (420°F) for 15 minutes or until done.

TARRAGON

Tarragon is one of the greatest of culinary herbs. There are two varieties, the superior being French, but probably Russian tarragon is more widespread. French tarragon is grown from root division or cuttings and likes a sunny position and light, well-drained soil.

Tarragon is an aromatic and is indispensible in *fines herbes* and sauces such as hollandaise, béarnaise and tartare. It blends wonderfully with chicken and pâtés, fish, shellfish and salads. The fresh leaf is essential, as it does not dry well. The delicate flavour enhances most savoury dishes.

Sauce Tartare

This is a traditional sauce for fish. I like it with boiled meats as well, as they sometimes taste a little bland.

1 egg yolk
1 teaspoon Dijon mustard
Salt and pepper
Olive oil
1 tablespoon tarragon vinegar
2 teaspoons chopped tarragon
1 teaspoon chopped sour gherkins
2 teaspoons chopped green olives
1 teaspoon chopped capers

Put the egg yolk into a bowl with the mustard and some salt and pepper. Add the oil drop by drop, stirring fast all the time until it emulsifies, then add the oil a little faster until the mixture is smooth and thick. Stir in the tarragon vinegar and add the chopped tarragon and the well-drained gherkins, olives and capers.

Refrigerate until serving.

Celery with Tarragon

This celery dish can be served as a dish on its own or as an accompaniment to a rich meat or fish course.

4 cups celery, cut into 6 cm (2¼ in.) pieces
1 tablespoon chopped tarragon
2 tablespoons chopped parsley
1 cup dry white wine
¼ teaspoon grated nutmeg
Salt and pepper
Soft breadcrumbs
2 tablespoons butter, cut into little sticks

Put the celery in a saucepan and cover with the herbs, wine and stock, nutmeg, and salt and pepper to taste. Bring to the boil, cover, and simmer for 15 minutes.

Take the celery out and arange it on a gratin dish. Pour the herb liquid over it, sprinkle with breadcrumbs and the butter. Bake for half an hour in a preheated oven at 180°C (360°F). Serve.

Tarragon Butter

An instant sauce for grills and barbecues to melt over the meats. Vegetables sautéed in the butter are excellent with the subtle taste of tarragon.

4 tablespoons butter
1 tablespoon white wine vinegar
3 tablespoons finely chopped tarragon
Salt and pepper

Cream the butter until smooth and gradually beat in the vinegar. Then add the tarragon. Salt and pepper to taste. Roll the butter into a long log and cut pieces off as you need them. Keep refrigerated.

Tarragon Chicken

1 chicken, free range if possible
½ cup tarragon leaves
1½ tablespoons diced pancetta or bacon
Pepper and salt
2 tablespoons butter
2 carrots, thinly sliced
2 onions, thinly sliced
3 cups hot water
1 tablespoon chopped tarragon

Wash and dry the chicken. Gently pull away the skin near the breast and legs and insert some of the tarragon leaves on both sides of the chicken. Put the rest in the cavity along with the pancetta and pepper and salt.

Melt the butter in a covered baking dish, add the carrots and onions and put the chicken on top of the vegetables. Cover and cook for 20 minutes in a preheated oven at 150°C (300°F). Add the hot water and some salt and pepper and cover again. Turn up the oven to 200°C (400°F) and cook for another 50 minutes or until tender.

Put the chicken on a serving dish and keep warm. Strain the vegetables off the cooking liquid and remove the fat. Add the chopped tarragon and boil down to half the quantity or until it is thick, stirring from time to time. Serve the sauce separately.

VARIATION: Add a dash of port or madeira to the sauce when the chopped tarragon is added.

THYME

THYME IS a powerful aromatic and one of the essential culinary herbs. It is grown by root division and requires a sunny position and light, well-drained soil. The most popular thymes are garden thyme, lemon thyme and caraway thyme. It has a pungent and warming aroma and taste.

Thyme is indispensible in bouquet garni, *fines herbes* and stuffings and is a background to many stews and soups of meat, fish and vegetables. It is a good roasting herb with lamb, beef, pork, poultry and game. Fresh thyme is much superior to dried.

Pork Chops with Apple and Thyme

4 pork chops
½ tablespoon chopped thyme
Pepper
1 tablespoon olive oil
1 teaspoon wine vinegar
1 tablespoon butter
2 cooking apples, sliced
¼ teaspoon chopped thyme

Marinate the chops in the ½ tablespoon of thyme, pepper, oil and vinegar for a few hours. Grill the chops, basting with the marinade occasionally.

At the same time melt the butter, add the apples and thyme, and sauté the apples until soft. Serve the chops and apples on warm plates.

Thyme Stew with Dumplings

An old-fashioned stew just like Grandma used to make. Dumplings are so delicious and easy to make I don't know why they have gone out of fashion.

1.5 kg (3 lb) chuck steak or similar
1 tablespoon flour
2 tablespoons butter
2 cups chopped onions
2 cups stock
Salt and pepper
1 cup chopped carrots
¼ cup chopped celery
1 swede, chopped
1 tablespoon chopped thyme

For the dumplings
1 cup flour
1 teaspoon baking powder
¼ teaspoon salt
30 g (1 oz) butter
1 tablespoon chopped thyme
1 tablespoon chopped parsley
¼ cup milk

Trim the fat off the steak, cut the meat into bite-size pieces and lightly dip them in flour. Melt the butter in a saucepan and add the onions and the meat. Brown the meat and onion all over. Add the stock, salt and pepper and, stirring gently, bring to the boil. Add the carrots, celery, swede and thyme. Stir, cover, then transfer to the oven preheated to 160°C (320°F) and cook for 1½ hours or until the meat is tender.

Meanwhile, make the dumplings. Sift the flour, salt and baking powder into a bowl and rub in the butter. Add the chopped thyme and parsley. Gradually add the milk until you get a wet dough. Makes 10 to 12 dumplings.

Twenty minutes before the stew is ready to serve, drop the dumplings into the stew. Make sure they sit on top of pieces of meat and not in the gravy. Cover and simmer for twenty minutes.

Serve with mashed turnips or parsnips.

Baked Thyme Vegetables

A lovely vegetable dish to accompany a roast or as a meal in itself. It is rather like a vegetable tart without the pastry.

2 tablespoons olive oil
1 cup sliced onions
4 medium zucchini (courgettes), sliced
2 small eggplants (aubergines), sliced
4 medium tomatoes, sliced
2 cloves of garlic, crushed
2 teaspoons chopped fresh thyme
Salt and pepper
3 tablespoons grated gruyère cheese

Rub a gratin dish with oil and spread the onion slices evenly on it. Make a layer of zucchini and cover with a little garlic, thyme, salt and pepper. Add the eggplant and then the tomato. Sprinkle the rest of the garlic, thyme and some salt and pepper over the dish. Dribble the olive oil over it and then the cheese. Bake for 45 to 60 minutes until the vegetables are cooked.

A very simple dish, baked thyme vegetables looks wonderful on the table and tastes just as good.

41

WATERCRESS

THE PUNGENT flavour and brilliant colour of watercress make it highly regarded as a culinary herb. It grows in or near water, from seed or by propagation. If you pick wild watercress, make sure the water isn't polluted. Store it in a bucket of fresh water.

Watercress is cooked as a vegetable the same way as spinach and accompanies roast and grilled meats and poultry. It is excellent as a salad and an ingredient in *fines herbes*. The flavour enhances soups, egg dishes, sauces and sandwiches.

Watercress Salads

Here are four ways of making watercress salad. They are excellent with rich meat dishes; their peppery flavour adds a lightness to the meal.

GRAPEFRUIT AND HAZELNUT
1 large bunch watercress, trimmed and washed
3 tablespoons hazelnuts

Vinaigrette
Juice of half a grapefruit
2 tablespoons olive oil
Salt and pepper

Make the vinaigrette by putting into a screw-top jar the grapefruit juice, oil, salt and pepper and shaking well. Put the watercress into the salad bowl with the roughly chopped hazelnuts and toss the vinaigrette over the salad. Mix and serve immediately.

BEETROOT AND OLIVES
1 bunch watercress, trimmed and washed
1 cup diced cooked beetroot
1 tablespoon olives, stoned

Vinaigrette
2 tablespoon olive oil
1 teaspoon lemon juice
Salt and pepper

Mix the oil, lemon juice, salt and pepper and shake. Toss with the watercress, beetroot and olives at the table.

ORANGE
As above, but substitute two oranges, peeled, sliced finely and halved, for the beetroot and olives.

APPLE
Substitute 2 sliced apples for the beetroot and olives, and add $\frac{1}{2}$ teaspoon of roasted cumin seeds and a dash of cayenne to the vinaigrette.

Watercress and Potato Soup

A simple but classic soup from France. The cream transforms the soup into the luxury class. Serves 4.

6 cups water
2½ cups diced potato
1 cup watercress leaves
6 tablespoons thick cream
¼ teaspoon grated nutmeg
Salt and pepper

Bring the water to the boil in a large saucepan, add the diced potato and cook until soft. Drain and mash the potato or put through a food processor. Put the purée back into the water and add the watercress. Bring to the boil and simmer for ten minutes. Add the cream and keep simmering, stirring constantly for about five minutes. Add the nutmeg, and salt and pepper to taste. Serve with some sprigs of watercress on top.

VARIATION: Mix a cup of yoghurt with a tablespoon of flour and substitute for the cream.

Watercress salad with beetroot and olives is a simple but delicious salad to serve with a rich main course.

Prawns with Watercress

1 kg (2 lb) prawns, cooked, shelled and de-veined
1 cup chopped watercress leaves

Vinaigrette
3 tablespoons olive oil
2 tablespoons lemon juice
2 tablespoons Dijon mustard
Pepper and salt
12 watercress sprigs

Combine the vinaigrette ingredients in a screw-top jar and shake well. Pour the dressing over the prawns. Serve with a few garnishes of watercress—enough for a few per serve.

MIXED HERBS

Fines Herbes

Fines herbes is a French term for the subtle mixture of parsley, chives, tarragon and chervil. The herbs are finely chopped together and used as a garnish for soups, egg dishes, sauces, and vegetable, fish and meat dishes. The mixture of herbs can vary— watercress is an excellent addition.

Fines Herbes Butter

220 g (7 oz) unsalted butter
2 tablespoons fines herbes (½ tablespoon each of parsley, chives, tarragon, chervil, finely chopped)
1½ teaspoons lemon juice

Mix the butter, herbs and lemon juice thoroughly. Form into a large roll and keep in the refrigerator to use as needed. Use it instead of a sauce to garnish fish and meat and toss with peas, new potatoes or any other vegetable.

VARIATION: Add watercress, finely chopped, garlic or spring onions.

Bouquet Garni

A bouquet garni is a little bunch of herbs tied together which is used to flavour stocks, casseroles and soups.

The classic bouquet garni is a couple of bay leaves and some sprigs of thyme and parsley tied together with string. A piece of carrot and a few celery tops are sometimes included; rosemary or tarragon can be added for chicken or lamb; stalks of fennel and lemon peel are ideal for fish dishes; the addition of orange peel goes well with hearty beef dishes. The bouquet is thrown out before the dish is served.

Mixed Herb Stuffings

Herbs make a wonderfully aromatic stuffing with bread or minced meats. Whether stuffed into chicken or turkey, cabbage or tomatoes, they enhance each other's flavour.

Chicken Stuffing

1½ cups stale bread, crust cut off
¼ cup milk
¼ cup diced and lightly sauteed onions
1 cup fines herbes (this page)
1 egg
Salt and pepper

Put the bread in a bowl and pour the milk over. Mix together; the bread will soon be soft crumbs. Add the rest of the ingredients and mix well.

Pork and Herb Stuffing

This is excellent for stuffing cabbage leaves, capsicums (peppers), eggplant (aubergine), zucchini (courgettes) and tomatoes.

30 g (1 oz) butter
2 tablespoons finely chopped onion
3 cloves of garlic, chopped
375 g (12 oz) pork mince
1 cup stale bread, without crusts
¼ cup milk
3 tablespoons fines herbes (page 44)
Salt and pepper

Melt the butter in a saucepan and add the onions. When soft, put in the garlic and pork mince and stir until it is lightly cooked.

Put the bread in a bowl and pour the milk over it. Knead until it is soft, then add all the herbs, salt and pepper, onions, garlic and pork mince. Mix well. Spoon into vegetables.

Rice Stuffing

1 cup finely chopped onion
2 cloves of garlic, chopped
2 tablespoons olive oil
2 cups cooked rice
1 cup water
3 tablespoons fines herbes (page 44)
½ teaspoon ground cinnamon
½ cup sultanas
Salt and pepper

Cook the onion and garlic in the oil until the onion is soft. Stir in the rice. Add the water gradually when needed. Add the rest of the ingredients and mix well. Cook until the water has evaporated, about 15 minutes.

VARIATION: Add 2 tablespoons of chopped dried apricots which have been soaked in water for an hour.

Rice stuffing tastes equally good stuffed into poultry or into vegetables such as zucchini, capsicums and tomatoes.

Herbed Sandwiches

There is no need to have butter on these delicious herb sandwiches.

4 tablespoons cottage cheese
1 tablespoon milk
Pepper and salt
1 cup fines herbes (page 44)
12 slices of bread, crusts trimmed off

Put the cottage cheese and milk into a food processor and blend until smooth. Mix with the herbs, pepper and salt. Spread on the bread and cut sandwiches into fingers or triangles.
VARIATIONS: Ham or shredded chicken can be added for a thicker sandwich; replace cottage cheese and milk with an avocado and a tablespoon of lemon juice; add chopped walnuts or olives.

Spicy Potato Filling for Pita Bread

Pita tastes much nicer warm, so put it in the oven or under the grill.

2 large potatoes, cooked and mashed
2 spring onions, chopped
2 tablespoons chopped fresh coriander
1 tablespoon chopped mint
1 tablespoon lemon juice
¼ teaspoon cayenne
1 teaspoon ground coriander seeds
1 teaspoon ground ginger
Salt

Combine all the ingredients and mix well.

Simple and delicious, spicy potato filling for pita bread makes an extra special snack or lunch.

Pasta with herbs makes a simple homely lunch.

Herb Omelette (Omelette aux Fines Herbes)

A classic omelette cooked in the French manner with the eggs still a bit runny on the inside. Speed is essential, so do not take your eyes off it while cooking Serves 4.

8 eggs
4 tablespoons finely chopped fines herbes
  (page 44)
45 g (1½ oz) butter
Salt and pepper

Beat the eggs and add the *fines herbes* and half the butter in small pieces. Season with salt and pepper.

Heat the rest of the butter in a pan; add the eggs. In just 30 seconds, start lifting the edges of the omelette so that the liquid egg will start seeping under.

As soon as the underneath is lightly browned, fold the omelette in two and serve.

Pasta with Herbs

500 g (1 lb) fresh tagliatelli
1 cup cream
60 g (2 oz) butter
2 tablespoons finely chopped oregano
2 tablespoons finely chopped chives
3 tablespoons finely chopped parsley
2 cloves of garlic, chopped
¼ teaspoon grated nutmeg
Salt and pepper
Freshly grated parmesan cheese

Put the pasta into plenty of boiling water and cook for 6 minutes. At the same time, heat the cream gently in a pan with half the butter. Stir the herbs into the cream along with the garlic and salt and pepper,

Drain the pasta and put into a warm serving bowl. Pour the cream mixture over the pasta and mix well. Put the remaining butter, cut into sticks, on the top with a sprinkle of parmesan and serve immediately. Serves 4.

47

INDEX

Page numbers in **bold** type indicate illustrations.